I SHOULD~~N’T~~ HAVE SAID THAT

Irreverent political and cultural commentary combined with humorous, poignant personal recollections.

Terry Feathers

Table of Contents

Introduction

For nearly 50 years I have been writing almost daily. Most of the time it was for others, and ranging from speeches, press releases, and radio ads, to campaign brochures, as well as, a stint as an editorial writer for the Kentucky Kernel student newspaper at the University of Kentucky.

But also, I wrote regularly for myself, from diary entries to journal essays and, in recent years, frequent social media posts. Sometimes serious, sometimes humorous, sometimes poignant but always unfiltered and with a certain disregard for political correctness. During the Covid pandemic, especially the times of lockdowns, I began writing more frequently as a diversion and as an effort to keep busy. I wrote with the hope that my feeble efforts might, in some small way, keep friends and family, if not entertained, at least distracted.

This book would never have happened without the encouragement of my friend Eric Semet, who more than once urged me to write a book. He seemed to think me a decent story teller. But to me the suggestion simply seemed overwhelming. I had never even considered such an effort.

It dawned on me, that given my years of writing, I had probably produced enough material to fill a book. So, I spent months sorting through a decade's worth of diaries, journals and social media posts in an effort to put together a collection of my favorite stories and memories. This is the result. Thank you, Eric.

I also want to thank my sister, Kim Feathers Caudell and my longtime friend Tim Buckles both of whom have been by my side through some tough times. And a very special thanks to my 'chosen family' at the Louisville Zoo, especially my mentors and teachers Angela Johnson and Sam Clites. They believed in me even when I had doubts. I can never repay their kindness and generosity.

Terry Feathers
Louisville, Kentucky

Chapter 1

2021

Jan 1 – What amazes me most about social media is that so many folks are so willing to put their ignorance and indifference on such public display. Daily I see some post and I think to myself, "I don't think I would have said that."

Jan 6 – Today's riot at the Capitol Building in Washington, D.C. has been deeply personal for me. It's hard to watch, especially through the tears. I committed 40 years to government service, from City Hall to the Kentucky State Capitol and one special summer in the mid-70s as an intern in the United States Senate. It was the summer of the historic Watergate Hearings and the office of Kentucky Senator Marlow Cook was in the Old Senate Office Building where the Watergate Hearings were held. In fact, on my very first day of work, I found myself on the sidewalk, waiting to cross the street standing next to prosecutor Archibald Cox. Over the following weeks I met the likes of Sam Ervin, Howard Baker, John Tunney, Edward Kennedy, George McGovern, Edmund Muskie, John Sherman Cooper and many others.

I got a personal, behind-the-scenes tour of the White House, sat on the floor of the House of Representatives along with other interns to listen to presentations from Congressman Gerald Ford and Senator Birch Bayh. And, I had the opportunity to walk onto the floor of the United States Senate (when they weren't in session). The history was so heavy you could feel it and the building is beautiful. The Senate Cloak Room and the Office of the President of the Senate are so beautiful they take your breath away. The Senate has been special and deeply personal for me since that summer. Today has been heartbreaking.

Jan 9 - It is disturbing to see so much hate exploding in our country, particularly when it's been egged on by people who know better just to serve their own ambitions and egos. But it occurs to me that so many of these "American individualists" actually hate their own mind-numbingly monotonous lives. They are essentially insecure and view themselves as failures and losers, even though they would never admit that.

And, because of their deep dissatisfaction with their lot in life and because of their unwillingness to accept any responsibility for their own situation, they find it easier to see themselves as victims and look for someone else to blame.

They blame some amorphous 'deep state' conspiracy to ruin their lives. This was never going to end well and those who tried to warn us were mocked or ignored.

Jan 12 - One summer I ran the historic 100-year-old carousel at the Louisville Zoo. As a result, I have come to believe that life is very much like a carousel. Sometimes you're up, sometimes you're down, but mostly you just go around in circles.

Jan 22 - Working at the Louisville Zoo was an amazing experience. Starting as a volunteer in the Animal Department assisting keepers in caring for the animals, preparing diets, and cleaning animal enclosures was a rare and enlightening experience. But working my way up to being hired as a Seasonal Keeper was beyond even my greatest hope. Yes, working with the lions, tigers and bears was thrilling and inspiring but my most lasting memory may well be working with an abandoned baby polar bear.

Qannik, which means Snowflake in the Inupiaq language, weighed less than 20 lbs. when found by oil workers on Alaska's North Slope in April 2011. With her mother nowhere to be seen workers contacted U.S. Fish and Wildlife, fearing the young bear would not be able to survive on its own. After an unsuccessful search for the mother, it was decided to rescue the cub and place it temporarily at the Alaska Zoo in Anchorage. Exactly what happened to the mother or why the young cub was abandoned remains a mystery. Some bear 'experts' theorized that the mother, who had been seen previously with 2 cubs, may have decided she was unable to provide and care for 2 cubs and chose to abandon one. But the truth will never be known. The young cub remained in Anchorage until June when a specially outfitted, climate-controlled UPS 747 transported her to her home at the Louisville Zoo, which had just completed construction of its new Glacier-Run state-of-the-art bear habitat and where I happened to be working as a volunteer.

When she arrived in Louisville in June 2011, she weighed in at around 65 lbs. Qannik was inquisitive, playful and enjoyed interacting with people. My favorite thing to do with her was to spread a little peanut butter and honey on the palm of my hand and press my flattened palm up against the heavy chain link partition of her enclosure. She would eagerly and happily lick peanut butter and honey through the chain link. How many people can say they've had a baby polar bear lick the palm of their hand?

Feb 7 - Truthfully, I've never been good or comfortable in social settings. At parties or other social gatherings, I've usually felt awkward and out of place. Now, after nearly 16 months of Covid quarantine, I'm not sure about comfortably "re-entering" social settings. It was hard enough before. Now it may be completely beyond my limited capacity.

March 4 - Honestly, I did fairly well academically in high school and college, but it never came easily for me. It was a real struggle at times and I even told myself on occasion that I must be stupid or certainly 'slow'. But I didn't discover the truth until I had a series of tests in my freshman year at the University of Kentucky. The tests revealed that I was dyslexic. That explained a lot, especially why I sometimes struggled with reading. Fortunately, it was a relatively mild form of dyslexia, but it was dyslexia nonetheless.

Over the past 50 years I've only told one or two people about this, not because I was embarrassed but because I didn't want to have to explain over and over what it was and how it impacted me on a daily basis. I've learned over time how to deal with it and I don't feel it has negatively impacted my life too much, other than the fact that I sometimes had to work a little harder than I really wanted. But, then again, maybe that was a good thing.

March 14 - Some folks like to think that others who live to be a certain age (70, 75, 80 or whatever) should just be grateful to be alive. I believe they think this because it's convenient and makes them feel a little better, but that's not really how it works. We all still need some motivation, some reason to get out of bed each day, even then life can still play havoc with us, can still throw that hard-to-handle curve ball our way. But the most important thing is not how many times life may knock us down, the more important thing is how many times we pick ourselves up, brush ourselves off and move forward, maybe a little bruised and battered and maybe a little slower, but still moving forward. That's what counts in the end.

March 15 - Okay, the doctor on TV just said: "There may be light at the end of the tunnel but we're not out of the woods yet." These are supposed to be smart, educated, professional people. Why can't they speak without the overused, tired clichés and mixing them at that?

March 23 - Just read that Prince Harry has a new job as a Chief Impact Officer, and I'm wondering, "What the hell is that?" I also read that the lady who has been serving as Harry and Megan's Chief of Staff has resigned. And I'm wondering, "They had a chief of staff?" And here's me thinking that just having a driver would be the bee's knees.

April 18 - When the late George Burns turned 95 years' old, he told Dick Cavett that he still smoked 3 or 4 cigars daily and had a martini with lunch and dinner every day. "What does your doctor say about that?" Cavett asked.

"He doesn't say anything," Burns replied, "He died 5 years ago."

May 3 - A Key West story told by Tennessee Williams:

Truman Capote, while drinking at Sloppy Joe's bar once autographed around a woman's navel. Her drunk, jealous husband pulled out his penis and asked Capote if he could sign it.

Capote looked at it and replied, "Well, I don't know if I can autograph it, but perhaps I could just initial it."

May 14 - In a recent survey of Americans, 60% said they were confident they could, unarmed, take on a grizzly bear and prevail. Some of you may recall that I helped care for several grizzly bears when I worked at the Louisville Zoo. All I can say is, IDIOTS. There are far more stupid people out there than I ever imagined.

May 18 – Explaining how math was used to count votes, Donald Trump said, "If you take one number and add another number to it, you get a totally different number. It's unfair and, quite frankly, a disgrace." I'm thinking Wharton must be very proud.

May 18 – It seems to me that I spend most of my time each day just searching. Searching for something I know I have, something I just saw yesterday, something I put in a safe place or something I cannot leave the house without. Whoever said 'seek and ye shall find' has never been to my house.

May 30 – I was very fortunate to be a part of the Louisville Zoo for nearly 5 years. And working with, caring for and feeding tigers, lions and bears was awesome and I made some of the best friends of my life, people that I miss every day. But the memory I cherish the most is what I would like to tell you about today, I was standing behind the building that houses the lemurs. I was waiting for my co-workers to meet up with me when a mom and dad and their 3 kids walked past me and headed down the hill. When they had gone about 15 or 20 feet past me, the little boy, who was probably about 7 or 8 years old, turned around and ran back to me. "Mister," he said, "do you work here?" "Yes," I answered. And, without saying another word he threw his arms open, gave me a big hug, turned and ran back to his parents. How many jobs get that kind of a thank you?

June 1 - There are literally millions of Americans out there who are disappointed and angry with how their lives have turned out. They haven't become famous, they're not wealthy, they don't live in large, luxurious homes, they don't travel to exotic places. In their minds, their lives are not personally rewarding and they don't see themselves as successful. AND, of course, it is not their fault, it couldn't be their responsibility, so, they find others to blame for their discontent. They blame government, they blame Asians, they blame blacks, they blame gays, they blame the educated. The "others", it has to be the fault of the "others". THIS is what has fueled the rise of the "grievance" politics of Donald Trump and his cult-like followers. Everyone is a 'victim'.

For decades we were a nation that truly believed "it takes a village".
Now, sadly, we are becoming a nation of "us and them".

June 11 - Americans have become extraordinarily lazy. Now, don't get me wrong, I'm not referring to physically lazy or too lazy to "get a job and earn a living" kind of lazy. That's a whole other rant on Entitlement for another day. No, I'm talking about the mental and intellectual laziness that seems to be exploding across the country. Think I'm exaggerating? Well, just go to the social media page of any local TV station, find a recent news story and scroll briefly through the comments folks have posted. What you will quickly find is that numerous folks have posted comments that make it obvious that they haven't even taken the time to actually READ the article they have chosen to comment on. Opinions more often than not stated as fact without any effort to read the article or actually gather the facts. It's just too much trouble, just too many tabs to click on, too much work.

July 5 - As far back as I can remember I've been a list maker. The 'To Do' list, grocery list, Christmas card list, yard work list, etc. But I have finally given up the 'lists', most of them anyway. They just weren't much help anymore. It may have something to do with the fact that I just keep losing them.

Aug 8 - Olympic Memories ... This has not crossed my mind for many years. Not many folks are aware that there is a youth sports program in the U.S. known as the AAU

Junior Olympics. Somewhere around 1968, give or take a year or two, I competed in a Junior Olympics qualifying track meet which I believe was held in Frankfort or maybe Lexington. Along with others from across the state, I competed to represent Kentucky in the long jump competition at the national Junior Olympics event later in the year. All I remember now is that I did fairly well, was pleased with the distance I jumped, but, in my age group, I finished just out of the top 2 or 3 who qualified to advance to the national competition. I've been kind of ambivalent about the Olympics ever since.

Aug 8 – The folks who seek out the expert advice and guidance of their 12-year-old about how to use a laptop, a new cell phone or a smart TV are the same folks who refuse the advice and suggestions of the most experienced, knowledgeable and best educated doctors in the United States. They gladly listen to the theories of their mechanic, the garbage man or the guy who mows their lawn. But, the man or woman who spent years in medical schools and teaching hospitals and has treated thousands of their neighbors, friends and co-workers couldn't possibly know more about diseases and how to treat them ... WE ARE SO SCREWED.

Aug 9 – Not many people are aware that while in college, I had a job interview with the Central Intelligence Agency.

Actually, I had 2 interviews. The initial interview took place on campus and because they were still interested, as was I, a second interview was conducted a couple of weeks later at a hotel restaurant in downtown Louisville. This would have all taken place in 1975 or 1976. It was a fascinating experience and a little unnerving as well. Eventually, we got to the nitty gritty which was they were looking for covert operatives, spies, they were looking for potential spies. It was made clear to me that it would be a potentially dangerous situation which, in some instances, might require me to take some type of violent action against others.

That alone did not really dissuade me, but on balance the pay and rewards just did not seem commensurate with likely danger involved, so the second interview turned out to be the last and looking back I think that was probably one of my better career choices.

Aug 12 - Social media, in many ways, has greatly damaged civil discourse in America. But all the rancor and rudeness is not entirely the fault of social media individual users, who through their behavior, should shoulder as much, or more, of the blame for the now dangerous divisiveness throughout our nation. During this pandemic, especially during the "lockdown" phase, social media provided many folks a much-needed diversion, an outlet to share an occasional essay, a personal rant or share a special memory.

I wrote, rewrote and edited essays and stories because it gave me something to do but also because I truly hoped I could provide something that might interest my family and friends and even, on occasion, make them smile or even laugh.

Aug 30 - When I first read that people were taking Ivermectin to fight Covid I thought it had to be some kind of mistake, I used to give it to my horse regularly to prevent worms. She hated taking it, obviously, she was smarter than a lot of humans out there.

Nov 4 - Now I'm not even a small-time celebrity being chased by has-been paparazzi, but I'm turning into a recluse none the less. Between pandemic issues, closed restaurants, dark movie screens, rude people and health challenges it's much easier, less challenging and more comfortable to just stay home, which seems to be what I do more and more these days. Some days that's a good thing and some days, not so much.

Nov 22 - Most folks would say that an inquisitive mind and a good education are assets and would serve you well in life. But I have a close friend who frequently tells me that I think too much. He says that I "over-think" things and often make them more complicated than they really are and, as a result, I worry more than necessary and more than is good for me. I'm worried that he may be right - but I need to think about it.

Nov 23 - One of the many sad things about growing old is that you've lived long enough to realize just how often people say things they don't truly mean.

Dec 6 - So many of these TV evangelists seem to forget that the real Jesus Christ was a long-haired, dark-skinned Jew who never spoke a word of English and whose parents were definitely NOT named Mary and Joseph. The real Jesus strived to comfort the poor, the sick, the homeless, the rejects of society. The real Jesus would have never said, 'you're a leper, you're an unwed mother, you're gay, get away from me. The real Jesus was gentle, loving and welcomed ALL.

The real Jesus hung out with prostitutes and lepers while denouncing the money changers and church leaders of the day. Too bad more of his self-professed followers today aren't more like the REAL Jesus.

Dec 22 - Media reports of the declining health of former University of Kentucky basket all coach Joe B. Hall brought to mind a story I haven't thought of in many years and one I've never told, at least, not that I can remember. Of course, UK basketball is a religion in Kentucky and when I first arrived on the University of Kentucky campus in 1972, Joe B. Hall had become the UK basketball coach but the legendary Adolph Rupp remained a major presence. He still had an office in Memorial Coliseum and could still be seen around campus.

It was widely known that Rupp loved Brookings restaurant on Euclid Ave. and would often have lunch there because, according to him, "they have the best chili in town". One day I was crossing the street at the intersection of Euclid and Woodland and a big brown Cadillac comes barreling around the corner driven by the 'man in a brown suit', Adolph Rupp himself.

I had to step quickly to avoid the Cadillac as it passed within two or three feet of me. All I could think was that my UK career nearly ended before it began and my name would have never even made the headlines.

Chapter 2

2020

Jan 2 - The "experts" are advising to stock up on necessities just in case you are stuck at home for a couple of weeks, Damn it, you don't understand, the store doesn't carry enough Little Debbies to last me for 2 weeks.

Jan 11 - Yes, I confess that I used to care (probably too much) about what others thought of me, until I realized that they really weren't thinking about me at all. What a relief that was.

Jan 15 - Today I was stunned when my doctor told me I was one of her star patients. I asked if that was a good thing or a bad thing. "Think about it," she said. "You've survived cancer, twice, you survived a heart attack and bypass surgery, you survived the worst form of c-diff infection and now you've survived pulmonary embolisms. Any one of those things, by itself, could have been fatal, but here we are and today's test results could not have been better all things considered."

Well, damn, I thought, *I need to celebrate.* So, I went to Krispy Kreme.

March 31 - My uncle Elmer. What a character he was. My dad, his 2 brothers and their sister, Rosie, were raised in poverty in the hills of West Virginia. When Elmer was about 16 years old, his Dad (my grandfather who I never met) sent him, on foot, into town to get some light bulbs. Elmer never came back. He left home, left West Virginia and began a journey worthy of a good look. Elmer was an outgoing person who had a loud and frequent laugh, a big smile and good heart.

Uncle Elmer did a stint in the Merchant Marines but ultimately ended up in Montana working on a large cattle ranch near the Canadian border. He became a real-life, working cowboy. His office every day was on the back of a horse. He often rode fences by himself for days at a time, checking for any breaks in the miles of fencing and spending nights sleeping on the ground or in the line shacks scattered along the way. Elmer eventually became a deputy sheriff in Montana and met a Cree Indian lady who had been raised on a reservation in Canada.

They fell in love and married, had several children, my cousins, and eventually moved back and settled in southern Indiana. After many years they divorced and all left the area. Over the years I lost touch with Elmer's wife and my cousins. But I did see my Uncle Elmer occasionally when he would visit my dad. In fact, Elmer, my Dad and I spent one chilly afternoon together fishing in western Kentucky and I am so glad we did because Uncle Elmer passed away not too many months later. Like I said, worthy of a good book.

April 16 - My social distancing efforts have been a miserable failure, No matter how hard I try I cannot stay 6 feet away from my refrigerator.

April 17 – In the early 70s I was fortunate enough to see Elvis in concert at the Kentucky Fair and Expo Center and I will never forget when he unexpectedly walked on stage in a white rhinestone-ladened jumpsuit and cape to join the great Carl Perkins in singing his classic Blue Suede Shoes.

April 20 – A few thoughts from a frustrated constitutional student with too much free time for my own good. So many folks are out there yelling about "my rights, my rights, my constitutional rights". But you don't have to listen very long to realize that they have never read the Constitution, never seriously studied or read of the history of the great struggles surrounding its origins and development and have certainly never studied the development of American constitutional law over many decades. Now, let me be very clear, I am certainly not an expert on any level, I wouldn't even label myself as highly knowledgeable, but for 50 years I have been an avid student of American government, its history and development and particularly the nature, character and personal and political agendas of the men who actually wrote and implemented our Constitution. It is a fascinating story.

The first thing I would point out is, that from the very beginning the Founding Fathers recognized that their Constitution was not perfect and almost immediately began amending and revising their own work. They were wise enough and, mostly, humble enough to recognize their own shortcomings.

The second thing I have noticed everyone seems to overlook, and any constitutional expert will tell you, there is no individual constitutional right that is absolute. Each right granted to citizens has some limit. The right of free speech is not absolute, there are some things you simply cannot say, e.g. yelling 'Fire' in a crowded theater when there is no fire and thereby endangering lives. The right to freely assemble is not absolute, e.g. cannot gather with intent to riot. The right to own a firearm is not absolute e.g. a convicted felon cannot legally possess a firearm.

BUT, the most important thing I want to highlight is that while everyone on every side is talking about their rights, everyone seems to be ignoring the other, equally important part of the American constitutional equation. Yes, we all have rights, more than most people in most countries, but we each also have responsibilities that come with those rights.

It brings to my mind the words of Benjamin Franklin, "We must all hang together or most assuredly, we will all hang separately." We really are all in this thing together folks. That's the most I've written in years.

April 24 – So, America, it has come to this, the government has to run TV ads to demonstrate proper hand washing and major companies have to issue warnings not to digest or inject bleach or Lysol – we are so screwed.

April 25 – Lord, I feel so old, there are way too many roads and buildings around Louisville that are named after people I actually knew or worked with.

May 6 - I wear a mask not because I live in fear of the virus. I wear a mask because I want to be part of the solution and not part of the problem. As for myself, I'd rather be a 'snowflake-sheep' wearing a mask than a 'whiner-crybaby' crying crocodile tears because I can't hit the bar or the bowling alley. But that's just me.

June 6 - Sorry to say that it is my nature to look at a situation and see the problems, the people I envy are those who can look at a situation and see the opportunities.

"I am not a pessimist, I'm a catastrophist." - Anderson Cooper
I have a lot more in common with Anderson Cooper than just white hair.

June 12 - I love good food and dining at nice restaurants. A long time ago I reached a point in my life where I preferred to do things rather than have things. It took me a while but I finally learned to value experiences and people more than possessions. I wish I had learned this lesson sooner. Two of my favorite things these days are the theater and dining out. But I regret that I have yet to enjoy many of the nicer eateries in our community.

June 26 - It's probably long gone by now, but many years ago in Key West, just across Duvall Street from the legendary Sloppy Joe's bar, where the likes of Hemingway, F. Scott Fitzgerald, Truman Capote and so many others have hung out over the decades, there stood a very large palm tree. This particular palm tree had an old, weathered and faded brass plaque that read:

ERNEST HEMINGWAY
pissed on this tree

July 15 – It is strange, the things you think and the things you do when you realize you may be facing a life-or-death situation. I remember vividly, 8 years ago, lying in the back seat of my mother's car, gasping for breath and realizing the chest pains were getting noticeably worse as my stepfather raced helter skelter through the suburban streets of Nashville to get to the closest hospital. I was desperately trying to make phone calls, one to the lady in Louisville I was dog sitting for, to let her know I probably would not make it back to Louisville any time soon, and one to my Zoo co-workers to let them know that I likely would not be able to start my summer job the next morning and, the most important call to my friend Eric because I wanted him to hear my voice and know that I was alive and conscious. I thought perhaps he would be less worried, but at the same time, with the chest pain almost unbearable, I realized it could possibly be the last message he would ever get from me. Fortunately, I was wrong about that part.

These past 8 years have been a real struggle at times, with many ups and just as many downs. But I've learned a great deal, especially about myself and it wasn't all pretty. But I have resolved, in whatever time may be left for me, to guide my life by new (for me anyway) principles. I will work to focus myself on the things that I have in my life and not the things I don't have. And, more importantly I will focus on the things I can still do and not mourn the things I can no longer do. Admittedly, it's a big change for me, but as I see it, it's the only way to move forward and I've never been one for standing still.

July 18 - Honestly one of the saddest things about this pandemic is that it has clearly demonstrated there are far more "cognitively impaired" folks out there than I had ever imagined.

Aug 3 - A couple of months ago I bought some of these wool dryer balls that are supposed to soften your clothes when you put them in your dryer. They seem to work fairly well except every time I open the dryer door the balls seem to hop out and roll off somewhere in search of Lord knows what and I have to go chasing after them.

Aug 17 - Over the years, in the deep recesses of my mind, I have formulated many plans for my life and God laughed. Of course, most of those plans came to nothing, but a few, a very few, actually came to fruition. And those "successes" all had one thing in common. Along the way there was someone who encouraged me, guided me, someone who took the time and made the effort to help me turn my plan into reality. I didn't do it by myself, none of us do it by ourselves, no matter what we might like to think. With all the challenges we face today, it is more important than ever before that we remember it really does 'take a village'.

Aug 18 – "Never argue with stupid people. They will drag you down to their level and beat you with experience." Mark Twain.

Aug 27 – "A house does not a home make." A cliché many of us have heard for years and, like most clichés, it has some kernel of truth at its core. It is something I have been thinking about for a couple of years now but have been hesitant to write about for fear of being misunderstood. Let me be clear, I have a place to live and in no way would I ever diminish the tragedy of those who don't.

But I am speaking in a philosophical sense not a physical sense about an aspect of being "homeless" that is often overlooked and seldom discussed but affects many in our society who, like me, have reached a "certain age". This aspect of being homeless I CAN understand because a home encompasses far more than just a house.

A home is a place where people are genuinely happy to see you and accept you as you are. It is a place where you feel valued, protected and safe, it's a place where no questions are asked, no judgements are made and no explanations are necessary. Home is a place where you can express your thoughts, opinions, your ambitions unfiltered without fear. This is the kind of place so many of us don't have and so many of us have never had.

Sep. 17 – For several months now I have been thinking a lot about anger, resentment and bullies. I have come to believe that the Coronavirus has not caused the anger as much as it has revealed resentment, even hatred, that has been lurking just below the surface for a long time now. And, it's clear this anger is not confined to any one group. It's not just conservatives or liberals, Republicans or Democrats, blacks or whites and it's certainly not only among young people but also those of us who are older as well and it may even be more prevalent among us "grumpy old people".

I have a theory about that, based on my own experience of 66 years. Many older folks, sadly, have actually come by the "grumpy" label after years, indeed decades, of being bullied, ridiculed or mocked by others. It often starts at a very early age when kids frequently make fun of other kids or call them names for any number of reasons ... maybe they have freckles, or they wear glasses, or they have braces, or they stutter, but whatever the reason this degradation often continues for decades. We all know about high school cliques and bullies.

The ridicule, name-calling and intimidation often continue into adulthood for 1,000s of different reasons. We all know those insecure, indifferent, uncaring people who are quick to mock or ridicule others because of their appearance or weight or height, age, accent or whatever the case may be. I know this from of my own experience. People, even in my adulthood, have tried to intimidate me or ridicule me because of my appearance, my height, my age or a dozen other reasons. Can there really be any surprise that a lifetime of such bullying and intimidation would produce so many "Grumpy Old People"?

Yours truly,
a " Grumpy Old Man"

Sept 28 – If it's true that Donald Trump paid his hair stylists $70,000, he certainly didn't get his money's worth.

Sept 29 - Went to the grocery store today to get some snacks to munch on during tonight's presidential debate. I should have gone to the liquor store instead.

Nov 3 - Election Day Thoughts - One thing I've learned for certain over nearly 35 years as a campaign staffer, manager, advisor and consultant, voters don't turn out in huge numbers or stand in lines for hours when they're happy about the way things are going. Voters turn out in huge numbers because they are pissed.

Nov 7 - For decades I've been fascinated by our Founding Fathers. Today Thomas Jefferson and John Adams have been on my mind. Please indulge me for a moment. In the aftermath of the presidential election of 1800, Jefferson and Adams (who had once been close) had a major falling out and did not speak to each other for a decade.

As they grew older and resentments cooled, they began an amazing and historic correspondence that continued until their deaths.

At one point Jefferson asked what Adams believed to be the most important character trait a person needed in order to live a successful, productive life. After an exchange of views, Jefferson noted that his experience convinced him that the single most important trait a person needed to have a productive life was not intelligence, not loyalty, not good humor. Jefferson concluded that perseverance and determination were the most valuable human characteristic. He believed that a truly determined individual would ultimately succeed even beyond those more gifted, more intelligent or more loyal.

Nov 20 – Many times in my life I've ended up on the losing end of one undertaking or another and I have learned one undeniable truth. It takes a person of character and strength to accept and acknowledge defeat and move on.

Dec 3 - Frequently I hear folks say, "I have no regrets, I wouldn't change a thing". And, I laugh, (usually under my breath) because I'm thinking to myself that person has lived and learned nothing or they are simply not telling the truth, maybe a little of both. Myself, I have many regrets, but not about career, success, power, money or fame, none of those superficial measurements of life. The regrets I nurture are the times I've disappointed people I cared about or respected. Often, I knew I'd been a disappointment because they told me so. Sometimes it was no big deal because they were people whose character and judgement I found to be lacking. But sometimes they were acquaintances, friends, even family who I truly cared about and did not want to disappoint.

I'm still a "work in progress" and hope I've learned from my shortcomings and have grown into a better, less disappointing, person. I kinda wish more folks would strive to do likewise.

<u>Dec 9</u> – Back before the 'PanDamnit' started I was talking (listening mostly) to an acquaintance at a local coffee shop. In passing, they informed me that they "liked old things that really had no use". "In that case, you should love me," I responded. They avoided me after that.

<u>Dec 20</u> - Watching Congress' chaotic scrambling to pass legislation before midnight in order to prevent a government shutdown brings old memories to my mind. Not too many years ago the Kentucky legislature faced similar difficulties in completing their legislative business before the midnight deadline imposed by the state Constitution.

Kentucky legislators came up with an ingenious way to get around the looming deadline. They simply unplugged the clock on the chamber wall. Those were the days.

<u>Dec 23</u> – I've devised a plan for the coming year. The next time I'm at the grocery store and some idiot runs into me with their grocery cart, I will immediately collapse on the floor in a lifeless heap.

Chapter 3

2019

March 10 – Seems like every day on TV I see folks say they can't wait for the day they can hug their grandkids, kids, parents, family, friends, etc. Often, they say it's the ONE thing they're looking forward to most. But, honestly, I'm not in that group. Yes, I'm old and probably grumpy, but the truth is, I've never been all that keen on hugging. It just, too often, makes me uncomfortable. Probably has something to do with my toilet training or some such thing, but I'm just not a hugger. Unless, it's a horse or a dog, those I could hug all day.

April 17 - Lord, I know it comes from the Bible and honestly I have tried ... but I'm too old, too jaded and too tired to suffer fools gladly or at all for that matter.

April 25 - The small Dutch island of Saba (population about 700) in the Caribbean is my happy place. It is a scuba diver's paradise. There are no big resorts and no white sand beaches. Saba is actually a dormant volcano and a marine preserve which makes it very popular with scuba enthusiasts. But getting there is not an adventure for the faint-hearted. The Saba airport has the shortest commercial runway on earth, and it is surrounded by water on 3 sides.

Other than diving, the most notable thing about Saba is the small offshore medical school located on the island. I always thought it somewhat ironic that the medical school was located directly across the street from the cemetery.

I traveled to Saba 4 times to do some diving and was never disappointed. There was always plenty to see: sharks, eels, rays, sea horses and more. But my most memorable dive had nothing to do with what we saw but rather what we did not see.

While diving one afternoon, my dive buddy, Robert, got my attention and began pointing to his ears. At first, I thought he was trying to tell me he was having trouble equalizing pressure as we descended. But soon I realized he was actually trying to tell me to stop and listen. The first rule of diving is you never stop breathing, but if you really want to listen for something you have to stop or, at least, slow your breathing. Robert was a much more experienced diver and I trusted him. So, I stopped breathing for just a moment and when I did, I heard whales singing back and forth to each other. The first and only time I've experienced that. We never saw them but we heard whale song the rest of the day. And what a wonderful day that was.

May 11 – "The mass of men lead lives of quiet desperation." Henry David Thoreau As I near my 65th birthday, I believe I'm finally beginning to understand what Thoreau was writing about. As we grow older, we don't have fewer worries, as we may have hoped, we just have different worries, different fears. We watch helplessly as those we care about most pass on. We face health challenges we never thought possible and the daily world in which we live becomes smaller and smaller. Honestly, none of my previous "milestone" birthdays have phased me, but 65 seems different, more real, bringing with it more worries, more uncertainties, more fear.

June 21 – Personally, I'm sick and tired of hearing people cry "that's not fair" about this or that. Life's not fair, never has been and likely never will be. Put your big boy pants on and deal with it.

June 24 – Only in the past few years have I come to realize that I've spent far too much of my life in the company of those who made me feel bad about myself. If those around you are quick to point out your mistakes, your failures and your shortcomings, they are not your friends. Your true friends are encouraging and supportive of the true you, regardless of your mistakes and shortcomings. They want to see you do well and be successful.

July 2 – I used to think I was a fairly smart guy, but the truth is I'm just a fairly well educated guy which is not the same thing at all.

July 4 – A few years back, while on an Alaskan cruise, I was lucky enough to visit a remote dog sled camp with 6 or 7 others from the cruise ship. After a tour of the camp and a brief presentation on training we were taken on a dog sled trip through the dense woodlands.

The dogs were energetic and very enthusiastic about running, in fact, they loved it. Of course, each dog had been handpicked based on their eagerness to run. As our group was getting into the van to return to the ship, we heard a loud commotion headed in our direction. We looked down the gravel road to see a beautiful Huskie running full speed right toward us. Close behind him were 4 or 5 guys chasing him and yelling loudly for him to stop, but apparently, he was not done with his running that day.

Instinctively, as the dog approached, I knelt in the middle of that gravel road and spread my arms open as wide as I could and I swear that dog ran right to me. The men trying to catch him stopped their running and their yelling. I have to admit that I was more than a little pleased with myself.

One of the men giving chase said to me, "I've never seen anything like that. How did you do that?" "I've always been pretty good with animals," I answered.

July 10 - Okay let me get this straight, Donald Trump called the British ambassador to the US a "stupid guy". This is the same Donald Trump who, during his 4th of July speech, proclaimed that George Washington's army protected our airports. Is it just me or is there something terribly wrong here?

July 25 - An old Cherokee told his grandson, "My son, there is a battle between two wolves inside us all. One is Evil. It is anger, jealousy, greed, resentment, inferiority, lies, and ego. The other is Good. It is joy, peace, love, hope, humility, kindness, empathy, and truth." The boy thought about it, and asked, "Grandfather, which wolf wins?" The old man quietly replied, "The one you feed."

Sept 23 - Yes, there is a Booger Bottom, Georgia. It is in Meriwether County in rural southern Georgia. It is a very small place and you will not find it on any highway sign and probably not on any map. I learned about it only because it was being discussed on one of the local radio stations I happened to be listening to while driving on I-75.

Sept 29 - When I was about 9 years old, friends of my parents who lived in Nashville got us all tickets to go to the Ryman Auditorium and see the Grand Ole Opry. This would have been the mid-1960s and the only performer I have a clear memory of was the iconic Marty Robbins (who sat at a piano in a sparkling costume that would have made Elton John jealous) and sang several of his biggest hits. Many years later after a multimillion-dollar renovation of the Ryman I saw Dolly Parton perform her first ever solo concert in the Ryman on that very same stage. What a journey it has been.

Oct 12 - Well, so far, I've only lost 3 things during my big move - the cord for my electric blanket, a box of (clean) underwear and my checkbook. Not sure which I should search for first.

Oct 14 - 10 years ago this week I was working as an extra on the Secretariat movie. I played a reporter and actually got a few fleeting seconds of screen time. We started very early, before sunrise, each morning. First, we had to report to Wardrobe, then Hair and Makeup and then on to a large holding tent to wait for our set assignments for the day. What an experience.

On the last day of filing at the Keeneland race track in Lexington, Kentucky I got to spend, quite by accident, the entire afternoon with Ron Turcotte, Secretariat's real-life jockey who was visiting the set that day.

Turcotte, who very nearly won the Triple Crown two years in a row (he won 2 of the 3 races aboard Riva Ridge the year before he rode Secretariat into sports history) is now confined to a wheelchair as the result of a racing accident. One of the movie's production assistants asked me if I would mind staying with Turcotte and seeing to any needs he might have while on the set. "Who do I have to kill to get that job?" I asked.

It was an amazing afternoon. Most of my time was spent either taking pictures of Turcotte with adoring fans, including some of the leading actors in the movie, or providing pens for him to fulfill the many autograph requests.

We spent several hours together talking, mostly me listening to him tell stories. But at one point a gentleman

I did not recognize but who appeared to be a retired jockey approached Turcotte and began speaking warmly to him in French.

After a moment Turcotte turned to me and said, "Terry, do you know this gentleman? He was a pretty good jockey too."

"No sir, I'm afraid I don't," I replied.

"This is my friend Jean Cruget. He won the Triple Crown too on a horse named Seattle Slew." One Triple Crown winning jockey introduced me to another Triple Crown winning jockey. How cool is that? Of course, I have both their autographs on a prop racing form used for the movie.

Oct 23 - There was a time when I made a real effort to look my best to try to make a good impression on others, but nowadays I try to look as good as I can so I won't frighten myself when I glance in the mirror.

Nov 10 - I had to change channels, that TV anchor lady was just talking a lot faster than I could listen.

Chapter 4

2018

Jan 6 - In the movie The Darkest Hour there is a scene where Winston Churchill gives a rousing speech to Parliament and one member says of Churchill, "He just mobilized the English language and sent it into battle." I think it highly unlikely that anything vaguely similar will ever be said of President Trump. He talks more like a 9 year old.

Jan 21 - Nearly all the choices we make in life have consequences, usually not terribly significant. Sometimes those consequences are good, sometimes, on rare occasions, they can be really good or really bad. I've certainly made more than my share of bad choices so I feel qualified to offer my observations and advice in this regard. It seems to me that making bad choices is only one aspect of the problem. Far too often the bad choice is born of spending too little time (or no time at all) considering the possible consequences of our choices before we actually choose. More time in consideration and reflection could result in better choices and fewer regrets… that's my opinion anyway.

March 16 - When you have cataract surgery you're not allowed to drive for several days. I was very fortunate to have a handful of generous friends who drove me to and from the surgeries and the follow-up doctor visits. What I learned during all this is that I kind of like being chauffeured around, it's much less stressful than driving yourself everywhere.

March 19 - Over the last 50 years I have worked with, for and against literally hundreds of politicians. And I can tell you one thing for certain, a true and dedicated leader does not seek out and does not enjoy confrontation.

March 28 - "Tough times don't last, tough people do." I've never really thought of myself as a tough person, largely I suppose because pretty much as long as I can remember, people have been telling me I'm not tough. Coaches and some teammates in high school told me I wasn't tough enough. I was beat up a time or two in high school and called some unpleasant names. I suppose I never looked tough, that's hard to do when you're barely 5'8" in your cowboy boots and I certainly never acted tough, I wouldn't even know how. But I think all those people must have been wrong and I must be tougher than I realized. Twice I've survived battles with cancer. I survived a heart attack and double bypass surgery and survived, barely, a deadly post-op infection that required removal of a large portion of my GI tract. If I wasn't tough before, these things have certainly toughened me up. I guess the point is you don't have to look tough or act tough to truly be tough. You really can't judge a book by its cover. Life's adversities don't change who we are – they reveal who we are.

April 6 – Recently, I read an article about "the most meaningful words anyone has ever said to you". Of course, that got me thinking, sifting through decades of memories, it was a good exercise. Things I hadn't thought of in years came into sharp focus, it was fun and moving. Of course, the most obvious and easiest answer would be "I love you." But that's too easy and often, too fleeting. After careful consideration, I settled on 2 phrases that moved me the most and have stayed with me over time.

A lady I once worked with told me one day that I was "inspiring" because of the way I was dealing with a recurrence of cancer. I was deeply moved and stunned because I certainly didn't feel inspiring.

But the words that have meant the most to me in my 6 plus decades are "I'm proud of you". I've only heard those words a few times and usually in relation to some difficulty or challenge I had to face but, for me, those words made all the difference.

<u>April 18</u> - The passing of Barbara Bush has brought into clearer focus a subject I had been mulling over in the back of my mind - how we face our own death. It's something most of us rarely talk openly about but nearly all of us have thought about at some point. We can only hope we handle it with the class and grace of Mrs. Bush. For me personally, after 2 bouts of cancer I have always thought it likely the cancer would, someday, return and I would be faced with the prospect of a 3rd struggle. But, I'm not at all sure I would opt for the rigors of chemo and radiation again. I suppose it would depend on the specifics of the situation, but I'm not sure it would be worth it. And, if that should happen, I'm not sure I would even share the facts of the situation with those around me. 'Comfort care' the Bush's called it, I like that.

<u>July 4</u> - Back in 1986 I got the chance to visit New York City for the centennial re-dedication of the Statute of Liberty; mostly I went because I really, really wanted to see the many tall sailing ships from around the world. It

was a once in a lifetime adventure and very impressive. While in New York I discovered a horseback riding stable a couple of blocks from Central Park. They rented out horses and, of course, there was no way I was coming home without riding through Central Park. Which I did one afternoon for a couple of hours. But the memory that has stayed with me for nearly 35 years was the number of little kids in the park that day who were so excited to see a horse and the many times I stopped and dismounted so they could pet a horse, some of them for the first time.

July 10 - Can't really explain exactly why, but I really enjoy watching the Tour de France. Maybe it's the beautiful countryside, maybe it's the accent of the British commentator, maybe it's the intricate strategies involved, maybe it's because I was once in Paris the day after the race ended and walked around all the grandstands and barricades on the Champs Elysees and realized just how huge an event it really is.

July 15 - It's hard to believe that it was 6 years ago today that I had a major heart attack while visiting family in Nashville. It has been a slow and difficult recovery, due in large part to the post-op infection I contracted, but here I am, still chugging along and looking forward to an upcoming trip to south Florida.,

Sept 26 – Politics aside, for a moment, forget Democrat/ Republican, conservative/liberal, isolationist/expansionist. What truly worries me about Donald Trump is that he exemplifies the segment of America wherein civility is no longer valued, indeed, it is reviled and mocked. Now, let me quickly add that I am equally appalled by so-called enlightened liberals/progressives/Democrats who also seem quick to abandon their civility. I would point to the hateful, sometimes disgraceful reaction to Kim Davis. And, don't think for an instance that I am defending her. Mr. Trump and a fair number if his supporters go far beyond rejecting political correctness, which, even I find sometimes has gotten out of hand. In the Trump universe it is perfectly fine to mock others, to call names and hurl invectives. It is okay to demean women using vile and disgusting language, it is okay to mock and ridicule a disabled citizen. It is even okay to call for the public execution of a political opponent, as some Trump supporters have done. This is NOT the America I was raised in. My parents and grandparents would have never dreamed of behaving this way and they certainly would have never allowed me to treat others in this way.

Now, certainly, this abandonment of civility was well underway before Donald Trump came along. But he has used it and played it up to a degree not seen in my lifetime simply to further his own agenda and ambition. It seems to me that a growing segment of our population is just fine with being rude, hateful, nasty, inconsiderate, and even vile, threatening and obscene when dealing with others on a daily basis. I do not exaggerate when I say this causes me great concern for the future of our society and, indeed, our country. If Mr. Trump truly wants to make America great again, he can encourage and lead an effort to restore some degree of civility and respect among all Americans rather than name calling, mocking and ridiculing of others that he seems to actually enjoy. But I'm not holding my breath on this score

Nov 4 – "The past is never lost to us . . . we carry it with us everywhere we go." When I was very young, I spent many of my summers at my grandmother's home in Cecilia, KY, just outside of Elizabethtown. My grandmother and grandfather lived in a very old farmhouse that had no running water, no indoor plumbing, and no telephone and was heated by coal-burning potbelly stoves. My grandmother's neighbors were a very kind, elderly and fairly sophisticated brother and sister. Everyone referred to them as Miss Jane and Mr. Gus. He was born in 1885, she in 1895 and they had a huge impact on my early life.

One day I had been playing in a recently plowed cornfield and came across an arrowhead. Being excited by my find, I rushed to show the arrowhead to Mr. Gus. Mr. Gus closely inspected the arrowhead and asked me if I liked cowboy and Indian things and of course I said yes.

He then proceeded to tell me that when he was a very young boy, about my age, his father had taken him to see Buffalo Bill's Wild West show when it was in Chicago. Yes, the elderly gentleman we all knew as Mr. Gus, the man I spent many of my lazy summers with, had actually seen Buffalo Bill in person – that still amazes me to this day.

But Miss Jane had her own amazing brush with history when she was a young girl. My aunt, Patsy Allen, who grew up living next door to Miss Jane, remembers Miss Jane one day telling the story of her own grandmother recounting how she, along with several others, had once been abducted by a band of local Indians. Although, uncertain, we are guessing this would have taken place somewhere around 1850. Eventually, Miss Jane's grandmother, along with several others managed somehow to escape as they were being marched back to the Indian encampment. They were able to make their way back home. Sometimes history is right in front of us and we don't see it.

My other vivid memory of my summers at my grandmother's house involved 'pig riding'. About 50 yards from Miss Jane's house was a small creek where I often played and explored. But a small portion, where the creek was very shallow, was fenced off to serve as a pig pen. Probably 10 or 12 medium-sized pigs enjoyed long summer days wallowing in and along the creek. My cousins, Steve and Eddie, and I would sometimes sneak down to the pig pen and try to ride the pigs. We would jump on their backs, grab their ears and hold on for dear life. Needless to say, the pigs didn't really like to be disturbed in this manner and would run and squeal like crazy. And, of course, they were quick and muddy and we were not able to stay on their backs more than a few seconds. But once thrown off into the mud, we had to get up quickly as the pigs would turn and try to bite us. I remember one afternoon in particular when the elderly, refined and usually subdued Miss Jane came out the back door of her house and yelled down in the direction of the creek, "You boys leave those pigs alone." Not a phrase you hear every day.

Dec 19 – I, for one, miss the stockyard being in downtown Louisville. Life was more interesting when we had cows or pigs running down the middle of Market and Main Streets during morning rush hour traffic. It certainly kept drivers on their toes.

Chapter 5

2017

Feb 14 - Over the past 45 years, I've been personally and directly involved in a good many hard-fought political battles. Sometimes I was on the winning side, more often, I was not. But never have I wished for or worked for the failure of the political victors. I have always wanted my city, my state and my country to do well, to prosper and move forward. I never understood those who publicly and loudly rooted for the failure of President Obama or President Bush, Not only is that self-defeating, it is, in my mind, un-American.

I did not support Donald Trump, but I did and still do, want President Trump to excel, to do a great job on behalf of the American people. But, I'm an experienced political realist and an aspiring political historian and I am confident of one thing at this point, our society quite simply is not prepared or equipped to survive for 4 years the chaos, confusion, disorganization and mean spiritedness of the past month. In this I include Democrats, Republicans, progressives and conservatives alike. "He who is without guilt…"

Feb, 18 - Recently I've been thinking lot about rhythm and tone, not really those having to do with music, but those having to do with life, your life, my life, the daily life going on all around us. It's something we see and experience every day, but not something we often give much thought to. Recently, I spent an enjoyable month back in Louisville. And, almost from the moment I arrived, I was struck by the difference in the rhythm of daily life in Louisville from that of south Florida.

It is a rhythm I know well, grew up with and am very comfortable with. We all know places like New York, Chicago and Miami have a more bustling, helter-skelter atmosphere than a Louisville, Cincinnati or Nashville. It's neither better nor worse, just different. But it struck me that just as cities have their own rhythm, each of us also has our own distinct rhythm of living, a comfortable rhythm all our own, and once we are able to get into that "natural stride", our lives become more relaxed, more comfortable, more enjoyable. Much of our lives, we are not really able to live at our own 'rhythm' because our workplace has its own rhythm, our friends have their rhythms and our significant others have their own rhythms as well. Sometimes, I think vastly different rhythms of life can present real challenges, especially in our personal lives.

As we get older, begin to retire, I think it's more important that we have a rhythm of life with which we are comfortable, more relaxed. After all, we have worked a lifetime and deserve to feel like we are where we want to be, living the life we want to live.

March 10 - Personally, I'm sick and tired of the phrase "entitlement reform". What they're really saying is they want to cut back Social Security, which is NOT an entitlement. It is an earned benefit as the result of years and years of regular payments from me and my employers. We paid in so we would earn the benefits down the road, Mismanagement by Congress does not change the fact that it is a benefit paid for by workers and employers. Do not let them get away with labelling it an "entitlement".

March 19 - Jimmy Breslin, a Pulitzer Prize-winning political columnist passed away today. He wrote one of the best political books ever, *How the Good Guys Finally Won*. If you want to know how politics really works, behind the scenes, this is the book I would recommend. He chronicles the behind-the-scenes maneuvering that eventually led to the impeachment and resignation of Richard Nixon. It is a fascinating story.

May 4 – Foolishly, I thought life would be less complicated in retirement, when, in fact, it's just a different set of complications.

May 7 – I am heartbroken today by the passing of Breeze, the most gorgeous Doberman I've ever seen. Breeze was a 95 lbs. chocolate Doberman who seemed to think that he was actually a 25 lbs. lap dog. He loved to lie on the couch, ride in the car and take long walks through the neighborhood. Early on he decided that it was his personal responsibility to protect me from all possible harm. And I always felt more secure with him by my side. He and his master, Eric Semet, have been my strength through cancer, heart surgery and so much more. He was by far the best medicine for my spirit. I will remember him for the rest of my days, thank you Eric for allowing him to be such a big part of my life and thank you Breeze for your love and devotion. Breeze was special in many ways. In my living room, in the cold winter months, I had one of those tower space heaters that rotated from side to side to blow warm air throughout the entire room. On particularly cold evenings Breeze would stand in front of that heater and move from side to side to follow the warm air. As I said, he was special.

May 12 – I would be willing to make a substantial wager that if you asked Donald Trump who Mark Felt was, he would have no clue. If you don't know who Mark Felt was, you might want to look it up. It is a piece of American political (and movie) history worth knowing.

June 1 – One of the things I've enjoyed most in my life is having a variety of friends who are significantly older or younger than I. It provides never-ending opportunities to learn new things and hear different perspectives. One of the more negative things I've noticed in south Florida is that older folks largely just hang out with other older folks, I'm not sure that's a good thing.

June 2 – What the hell is wrong with people? I see Jeff Corwin called our withdrawal from the list of nearly 200 nations who had agreed to the Paris climate agreement, "outrageous" and "shameful", and immediately he is attacked, ridiculed and called a variety of names on social media by the "non-believers". We have become a boorish, nasty, hateful society when you see a noted, educated, widely-respected 'expert' viciously and personally attacked because he speaks out on the very subject he has spent a lifetime studying and working on. I hate to say it, but I fear we have degenerated beyond any conceivable redemption. We may not even be worth saving. To say that I'm disheartened would be an understatement,

June 3 - Listening to Phil Collins and reliving the 80s. Some good times. Listening to these songs takes me back to places and people, some who are no longer with us and fills me with joy and sadness and wonder about what might have been.

June 21 - "How are you doing?" is the question people ask me most often these days and the truth is I'm never quite sure how to answer. In large part because I don't think most folks would like a brutally honest answer. In recent years, several friends have told me that I am a fighter and how impressed they are by my strength and toughness. Such kind expressions are always appreciated and often, sorely needed. But the truth is, I don't feel strong or tough, not at all.

Most days, rather than tough or strong, I feel completely overwhelmed, even defeated at times, but I keep going, more slowly than I used to, but still moving forward, it's what we do, what we all do and I know many of my peers and friends have quietly faced much harsher challenges. 'Endeavor to persevere' with a little grace and dignity, it's all we can do really.

Aug 7 - It was 5 years ago today that I finally left the hospital in Nashville after double bypass surgery and barely surviving a post-op infection. I wish I could say that I'm doing well, but that would not quite be the truth. I do have some good days for sure but also have some that are not. But through all the difficulties I have leaned on a handful of friends and family who have supported and encouraged me, who have given me a reason to get out of bed, most days anyway. Far too often we forget just how important the people around us are, we forget that they have their own difficulties and challenges, we forget to say thank you for all you have done and continue to do.

Sept 4 - Looks like I may have to cut my Louisville visit short and drive nonstop back to Fort Lauderdale to undertake hurricane preparations. Forecasters are saying Hurricane Irma, a Category 4 storm, is bearing down on south Florida.

Sept 12 - Goodbye Hurricane Irma, a Category 4 with winds over 100 mph. I am fine, my apartment, which is about 100 feet from one of the many canals in Fort Lauderdale, did not flood and was not damaged by the wind. I rode out the storm a few miles inland with a friend and his dog and they are fine as well. Several times we all huddled in the dark in an interior closet due to several tornado warnings in the area. Right now, I'm about as exhausted as I can ever remember being! Maybe later I will share my story of driving 16 straight hours from Louisville to get back here and immediately begin preparing for the storm and what it was like to face a Cat 4 Hurricane Irma right now I just want to sleep.

Sept 13 - Okay, still a lot of work to do, actually, a lot of work to be undone. I live right on the inter-coastal waterway in Fort Lauderdale. If you were to walk out my front door and turn right, the inter-coastal is about 30 yards in front of you. There are some docks and very nice boats that are always fun to watch. I spent 2 full days preparing, rolling up rugs and placing all my furniture up on blocks, bricks, paint cans, whatever I could find, to try to protect it in case the water got into my first-floor apartment. I sorted and prepared food in case we lost power or in the event I was forced to evacuate and I packed several suitcases with clothes, medicine, etc. and loaded them into the car, to be ready for a quick exit. Now, all that preparation has to be undone, not that I'm complaining mind you, but there is work to be done even though we were fortunate this time. But the thought of having to do this every fall is not altogether appealing. But, at least, I won't be wondering how I'm going to spend my weekend.

Sept 14 - Life is just inexplicably strange sometimes. Today I have been putting furniture, rugs, plants, etc. back in their proper places, post Hurricane Irma, I sit down for a short break, turn on my TV and not only are they showing the movie Secretariat, but it is the scene in which I actually appear on screen; it's strange to unexpectedly see yourself staring back at you from your television screen. Well, of course, I had to watch the remainder of the movie, I haven't really seen it in several years. The closing scene, with Secretariat winning the Belmont by 30 lengths is really very moving.

Sept 18 - Tonight, someone special is gentle on my mind and that brings a smile to my face but also a tear to my eye because I can't help but wonder what might have been.

Oct 4 - I have to admit that I find it just a little bizarre that there's a limit on how much Sudafed you can buy, but you can get all the guns and ammo you want, Something in there is not quite right,

Dec 15 - This has been a defining year in my life. The decision to return to Louisville after 3 years in south Florida was agonizing and difficult, And, I wasn't certain how I'd feel about returning, but I have to say that being back in the historic Highlands neighborhood feels very comfortable, whether it's Day's, the Bristol, Kashmir, the Mid-City Mall, Twig and Leaf or the Zoo, it is my happy place, comfortable and welcoming, just the right rhythm for this stage of my life.

Chapter 6

2016

Feb 17 - Without doubt the best live stage performance I have ever seen was the late Hal Holbrook in his award-winning show 'Mark Twain Tonight'. I've seen it 3 times over the years, the last time was just a couple of years ago in Evansville, IN. and I was lucky to snag a front row seat. Holbrook first performed his one-man show back in 1954 and eventually took it to Broadway where it earned him a Tony Award as Best Male Actor. He continued to perform it until 2017.

March 24 - Okay, this past Tuesday was a big day for me, a milestone really. It marked 90 days before my 62nd birthday. What's the big deal about that you may ask. Under federal rules, that was the first day I could apply for my Social Security retirement benefits and apply I did. So, now it's official, I'm old but glad to have made it this far.

April 4 - With a great deal of interest and amusement, I've been watching all the speculation about the upcoming Republican National Convention. I was very lucky to be a Delegate to the Democratic Convention in Atlanta back in 1988, along with my friends Margaret Walker and David Karem. It was an amazing experience. I got to meet John Kennedy, Jr., John Glenn, Olympia Dukakis, Bill Clinton, Al Gore and many others. What great memories.

April 9 - Okay, here's the deal, I love the theater, pretty much all theater, thanks to Jon Jory and his father Victor and teachers back at Suda E. Butler High School in Louisville who took us on a field trip to Actors Theater of Louisville to see Death of a Salesman, starring the great Victor Jory when I was in the 7th or 8th grade. Since that day, I have loved the theater. I've always wanted to tell this story to Jon Jory but never got the chance.

May 21 - In just about a month, I will turn 62, I don't mind admitting that. On the whole, I think I'm doing fairly well for 62. But, recently, while in a somewhat reflective mood, I thought to myself that never in a million years did I ever think I would be 62 and still single but, on further reflection, I realized I never even thought I would ever be 62. Just goes to prove that reflection is not always helpful.

June 3 - Muhammad Ali, a true Louisville legend, the original "Greatest of All Time", passed away today. He was the only man to win boxing's Heavy Weight Championship 3 separate times and was genuinely a larger-than-life character, physically and figuratively. I can clearly remember the first time I met him. It was 1979 and I was working for the Louisville Board of Aldermen on the Third Floor of City Hall. Word spread throughout the building that Ali was in the Mayor's Office on the first-floor meeting with his friend and Louisville Mayor Dr. Harvey Sloane.

A handful of staffers quietly slipped downstairs to hangout in a small waiting area just outside the Mayor's office to get a close-up look at Ali. When the door opened and he walked out I was stunned by his sheer size. He filled the doorway; his shoulders brushed the door frame on each side and to say he was solidly built would be an understatement. When he saw our group waiting to see him his face lit up and he became animated, smiling and playful, full of banter for his obviously adoring fans. He was there to have a press conference with the Mayor and another Louisville Heavy Weight Boxing Champion Jimmy Ellis. Hard to imagine meeting 2 Heavy Weight Boxing Champions in one room. Of course, I got Ali's autograph and to this day it is one of my most cherished possessions.

June 19 - This week will mark a significant milestone in my life. I will become eligible for Social Security retirement benefits. Now, to me, that screams OLD, it is definitely better than the alternative. But it also raises a whole series of questions that, frankly, I have been struggling with and, I dare say that many of you around my age have also faced: "What do I want to do with the rest of my life? What would my 'good life' look like? What would it feel like? And, where would I feel most comfortable living my 'final years'?"

Right now all I have are questions, doubts and even some fears. The certainty and confidence of youth seem to fade with the years. But I know there are a handful of people out there who mean the world to me no matter what.

June 22 - A Facebook post today, my birthday, by my friend Eric Semet. It was encouraging and deeply appreciated.

"Today is Terry Feathers' birthday. He doesn't think so but he is a fighter. To beat cancer twice, be in a coma for a week, having your kidneys shut down, losing over 40 lbs then slowly and painfully, very painfully at times going back up a slope, I call that person a fighter. Happy birthday Terry, you could teach us a thing or two."

July 26 – Honestly, you probably don't want to know my thoughts about this presidential election and I'm okay with that. Because the way I view politicians, politics in general and campaigns specifically is radically different than most of my friends and family. Politics has been my life's work since 1968, that's no exaggeration. I have known hundreds of politicians and candidates from city hall to the state capital to Washington, D.C. I've seen them at their best and their worst, I've seen their public faces and their private insecurities. Since 1968, I've worked in over 50 political campaigns all the way from school boards, city councils, state legislatures, judicial campaigns, gubernatorial and congressional campaigns and even presidential campaigns. I've worked as a lowly volunteer, an organizer, a paid staffer, campaign manager and as a campaign consultant on dozens of campaigns.

This experience over 45 years gives me a perspective that is quite different than that of most folks, not better necessarily, but certainly different. I don't see politics and politicians as inherently evil and I don't believe they are all crooks or liars. Those are the views of those too lazy to do the necessary research and thinking in order to come up with an educated and reasoned opinion,

Politics is too important to be left to the uninformed, uneducated voter, although that is exactly what usually happens. Politics is one of those subjects where everyone has an opinion whether they know what they are talking about or not. I gave up a long time ago trying to persuade or convince others of the rightness of my political views, I'd rather just run the campaign, it's usually easier.

Aug 14 - Probably the single best concert I have ever seen was Dolly Parton at the Ryman Auditorium in Nashville years ago. She sat on a stool center stage and for nearly 2 hours sang the classic songs she had written over the years, introducing each one by describing the person, event or story that had inspired her to write the song in the first place, I have never seen anything like it, before or since. What a talented lady.

Aug 17 - While it is true that we are all entitled to our own opinions, regardless of how ill-conceived or ill-informed they may be, that does not mean we are entitled to our own facts. And, as the late Hubert Humphrey so aptly pointed out, our right of free speech does not come with a guarantee that others will or have to listen to us, that depends on the value and quality of what we have to say.

Sept. 30 - On this day back in 2009 I was an extra in a scene with John Malkovich, Diane Lane and Nestor Serrano, and that same afternoon I spent nearly 4 hours with Ron Turcotte, the real-life jockey who rode Secretariat to the Triple Crown championship. What an amazing day that was.

Oct 8 - I'm old and I'm slow, it's true. All these years I thought I loved Van Gogh because of the color and energy of his paintings, but that's not it. Only today did I realize that Van Gogh did not paint what he saw. He painted what he FELT and that is what I love about his work. Better late than never.

Nov 21 - This has been on my mind and for a while, it's complicated. But, as we grow older it is normal for our universe, the world we personally interact with each day, to shrink, to become smaller. I tend to think this is a bad thing, but age, retirement, mobility and health issues often give us little choice but to cut back. For me, moving to south Florida was, in part, an effort to expand my universe or, at the very least, prevent it from shrinking too much after my retirement and health challenges. The effort has not been as successful as I had hoped. I failed to realize how difficult it can be once you reach a "certain age" to create a new life for yourself, especially when you are 1,000 miles away from lifelong friends, family and comfortable surroundings. But that doesn't mean I will give up pushing the boundaries of my comfort zone, not yet anyway. Now, I have debated with myself whether to post this, I'm not complaining or seeking solace. But

I know some of my peers are facing similar situations with varying degrees of success and I know some of my slightly younger friends will be dealing with this in the near future and I thought perhaps this might be of some small help. Keep pushing the boundaries and stepping outside your comfort zone as long as you're able and then do it some more. Don't settle, there will be time to be comfortable, later.

Dec 17 - Haven't been able to stop thinking about this, so I'm hoping if I write this, I'll be able to put it behind me. We all have dreams, things we desire and dream for. When we are young, we may dream about that perfect Christmas present we must have. As we mature, our dreams usually change and mature as well. Maybe we dream of the perfect car, house, vacation, the perfect job and, of course, the perfect life partner. All fairly common and understandable desires. But dreams are funny things, what we can't live without today may hold little interest next week. And, even when we do achieve some personal dream, we often find that it doesn't really measure up, it doesn't provide the joy and fulfillment we had envisioned.

I was fortunate that my dream of having my own horse, which I was able to do back in the 90s, was as great a joy as I ever imagined and my dream of learning to scuba dive, also achieved in the 90s, was every bit as exciting and wondrous as I imagined. These were dreams I'd held on to since my early childhood; dreams I'd never given up on over the decades, despite learning the hard way that dreams realized don't solve all our problems or make life perfect and easy. Even this realization doesn't and shouldn't prevent us from dreaming, from trying to make our lives fulfilling and enjoyable. Although, now retired, I'm still chasing another long-held dream of living near the ocean. The jury is still out on just how fulfilling that is. But the important thing is that we keep chasing those dreams, whatever they are, as long as we are able.

Dec 21 – Those of you who know me know that I'm something of a history buff, particularly American political history. It's in that vein I offer the following. It is not offered as a political statement in any way, except to note that now, for the 5th time in our nation's relatively young history, we will have a president who was not the choice of the majority of voters. While the idea of an Electoral College may have been a good compromise at the time, in order to 'protect' smaller states, especially slave-holding states, I think it has outlived its usefulness in this day and age. It should not be particular states that decide the presidency, after all, states don't actually vote. It's individual voters who vote and each of their votes should count equally. The only way to accomplish that is to move toward a "pure democracy" with respect to our presidential election, which means a direct vote of our citizens to choose our president.

Dec. 26 - It has always confounded me that we never recognize the best moments of our lives when they are actually happening. We only recognize them upon reflection, such a shame.

Chapter 7

2015

Jan 1 - I start a new year with a new home in a new state, a whole new life really, at the very least, a brand-new chapter in my life. It's been a long time in the planning and I am excited about the new possibilities, I think this is going to be a good thing for me and I plan to take full advantage of the opportunities south Florida has to offer.

Jan 29 - First day as an Animal Department volunteer at Flamingo Gardens ... cleaned and prepared exhibits for 3 Florida panthers and a bobcat, raked and cleaned the flamingo yard and hand-fed several brown pelicans. All in all a pretty good first day. Still hard for me to believe I'm living and working in south Florida.

Feb 7 - Despite the fact that nearly everyone proclaims the importance of a good education for their kids, grandkids, etc., there are growing numbers of folks who seem to enjoy ridiculing and denying the very empirical, scientific truths that the 'education community' has discovered and revealed through many, many years of hard work, research and testing. Now, I find it strange that most of these folks will not deny the scientific findings relating to such things as cancer, heart disease, stroke, etc., but these very same people, including way too many supposedly educated politicians, including Rand Paul from my home state, are so fast and fierce in their denial or questioning of the science behind climate change and now, of all things, childhood vaccinations. I'm sorry, but these people are not just idiots, they are dangerous idiots and if they persist in this ridiculous pandering to an angry, bitter few, then nothing they say should ever be taken seriously by anyone.

Feb 10 – It may just be that I have stumbled into a whole new career here in south Florida. Last week I went to this very nice lunch for seniors new to the Ft Lauderdale area, everyone was very friendly and the food (Italian) was excellent. Once they heard that I had worked at the Louisville Zoo, they asked if I would speak at next month's luncheon. They want me to speak for about 15 minutes on zoos and what it's like to work at one. I'm just hoping they have Italian again.

Feb 13 – Okay, I admit it was kinda cool to meet "The Rock", Dwayne Johnson today. He was very nice and very big. He was at Flamingo Gardens today filming an episode of a new show for HBO. BUT that was not the coolest thing I did today. This morning I got to hand feed Josh, a Florida black bear, He did really well, especially as I was totally new to him. I never get tired of working with bears.

March 15 - Yesterday I gave my lunch-time presentation on zoos to a group of nearly 50 retired folks. It went well. I enjoyed it. Everyone was very enthusiastic and had tons of questions, it was a good afternoon. Then last night had a great dinner with good friends at a waterside restaurant out on Key Biscayne. Life's good.

April 16 - We spend so much time and effort trying to build strong careers and so little time or effort building strong character. Author David Brooks calls it 'resumé virtues vs eulogy virtues'. I've been thinking about this a lot because I know that I am certainly guilty of making career building a higher priority than character building. Maybe it is a mistake we only recognize with age, but it is a mistake I greatly regret. But as Brooks points out, it's never too late to start.

April 22 - There are so many 'negative' people out there everywhere who seem to live only to point out the mistakes, shortcomings and flaws of others. They complain incessantly about anyone and anything and I, for one, am fed up with all the complaining and criticizing. I say put more thought and effort into making your own life better rather than running down that of others. Have a great day.

May 1 - In the late 80s I stumbled into one of the most wonderful fulfilling experiences of my life. Even though it involved some pain and a couple of broken bones. I had always loved horses for as long as I could remember. Around 1989 I was fortunate, with the help of a good friend, to find Star, a beautiful bay pleasure horse. A bay is essentially a brown horse with a black mane and tail and black legs. Star was beautiful, smart and well-tempered most of the time. I saw her every day, spent as much time with her as I could and I would take her for leisurely rides every weekend through the nearby park, weather permitting. We developed a strong bond and she would get excited when she would hear my voice outside her barn. But Star came at a price. When her health began to decline, I was devastated, but even long before that she would prove costly in another way. While searching for a suitable horse to buy, I looked at a horse owned by my friend John. As he was showing me the horse something spooked her. She spun around quickly and kicked me squarely in the chest with her back hooves. She knocked me to the ground but I quickly got up and said, "I'm okay". But I clearly wasn't okay and just as quickly passed out in a heap on the ground. Turned out I had 3 broken ribs. I did not buy that horse. John later told me that it took him almost a month to train that horse to do that.

May 2 - Its Kentucky Derby Day in Louisville and it always brings back a flood of memories for me; the year I saw Steve Cauthen win aboard Affirmed, the year I got to see Elizabeth Taylor and, of course, the year it snowed. I was at all those Derbies. What great memories.

June 1 - Harvard Yard, on the campus of Harvard University in Cambridge, Massachusetts, holds many wonderful memories for me and a few not so wonderful. I was fortunate and a little surprised to be admitted for summer classes at Harvard in the summer of 1975. I wanted to study government and figured there was no better academic setting than Harvard.

It was a heady and exciting summer of daily classes on government and American political history, a lot of studying but also a fair amount of exploring the history and culture of Cambridge and Boston and an occasional trip to the beach. Early on, while playing flag football in "the Yard" with some roommates, I managed to break an arm while diving for a pass. I spent the rest of the summer in a cast. But that did not slow me down much. And I did catch the pass. The collision of Kentucky and New England accents was amusing and confusing. But we all muddled through without much damage. And, I even managed to come away with pretty decent grades. The majesty of the historic dining halls still amazes me to this day. They were straight out of Harry Potter. I still managed to catch the Boston Pops for their customary July 4th concert on the banks of the Charles River and watch the Red Sox in historic Fenway Park. It was a great summer when all things still seemed possible.

June 22 - Honest, there were a couple of times I thought I might not make it to my 61st birthday. It's been a challenging, but nonetheless, I am here, if I had known I would make it to 61, I would have taken better care of myself. Happy birthday to me.

July 2 - Family stories have it that back through the mists of time, among our ancestors were a smattering of Cherokee Indians and that, in fact, is where the family name of Feathers comes from. Many of my Facebook friends probably are not aware that for several years I was honored to sing with an American Indian drum group, actually a couple of different drum groups. We performed throughout Kentucky, Indiana, Ohio and Tennessee at pow-wows, festivals, schools, libraries, universities, etc. It was a wonderful time in my life. I made memories and friendships that I still cherish today.

July 24 - Sen. Ted Cruz called Kentucky Senator Mitch McConnell a liar, on the Senate floor today. That is pretty much unheard of - that a senator would call his own Majority Leader a liar, on the floor of the Senate, WOW!

July 28 - Tonight's speaker at the Guest Speakers program I attended was a little out of the ordinary. I've seen lots of speakers over the years ...Bob Woodward, Hubert Humphrey, Gerald Ford, David Sedaris, Jeff Corwin, Julian Bond and many more. This was one of the most unusual and one of the most entertaining. I laughed all night; he was a 70s icon whose name few would recognize. It was Randy Jones, the original 'Cowboy' from The Village People. He was very interesting, very articulate (he's a graduate of the University of North Carolina) and he was a ton of fun.

Aug 23 - They say confession is good for the soul. I have not gone to the beach a great deal since I moved to south Florida because I am embarrassed by all the scars I have from my many surgeries, plus the fact that I have lost so much weight. When I told this to my friend Eric, he told me that I should not be embarrassed because they are the scars of a warrior, a warrior who has survived. He can be very insightful at times.

Aug 26 - Ok, I definitely have a new favorite grocery store. It's a Winn Dixie on Ocean Drive in Fort Lauderdale Beach. When I walk out the door and look to my right, I can see the ocean; that makes grocery shopping so much more enjoyable.

Sept 1 - "When you dance your purpose is not to get to a specific place on the floor, but to enjoy each step along the way." Life is about the journey.

Sept 11 - "You can never be over-educated or overdressed." Oscar Wilde. I've commented on this before, it seems that there is an anti-intellectualism growing in this country and that is a scary and dangerous thing, I for one would like an America with a lot smarter people in it.

Sept 20 - "If you want to go fast, go alone. If you want to go far, go with others." Pope Francis. How insightful and profound. I wish someone had said that to me when I was much younger.

Oct 2 - These political 'leaders' who continually want to shut down the federal government over this issue or that issue complain that it is their only option (despite the fact that their party controls Congress). It's their only option because they are unwilling to even consider the possibility of some type of compromise. These self-described "strict constitutionalists" are either stupid or just hypocrites (or both). I say this because they either do not know much about American history or they simply choose to ignore it. If our Founding Fathers had not fully embraced the art of compromise, our very Constitution almost certainly would have never been drafted nor adopted.

<u>Oct 25</u> - It is my guess that I am not the only one who has experienced this. It seems to me that the older I have become, the more emotional I have become. Recently I was watching some documentary film from 1968 and I noticed as I was recalling those days my eyes began to tear up and I could not figure out exactly why. Of course, retirement and the ending of a working career brings an explosion of emotions. I think it must have been a combination of the hope and optimism of those teen years and the stark realization that more of my life is behind me now than is ahead of me and that is always a sobering realization.

<u>Nov 26</u> - Thanksgiving was one of my favorite days to work or volunteer at the Louisville Zoo. It is closed to the public but the animals still have to be fed and cared for.

So, the Zoo is unusually quiet and calm, it's a very special place and time.

Dec 5 – "Strength is built by one's failures not by one's successes."

Dec 14 – Holcomb, Kansas ... It's highly unlikely you have ever heard of Holcomb, Kansas, but not only have I been there but it is one of the most enduring and vivid memories of my life. Somewhere around 1965-67 my parents, my grandmother and I took the family "vacation from hell" and drove from Louisville to Los Angeles and back. Along the way, my mother was adamant that we make a side trip to Holcomb, Kansas. Why? You would be justified in asking.

Truman Capote, a year or two earlier in 1965, had published his blockbuster best seller *In Cold Blood* which my mother had just read. The book (an addictive read) was based on actual events and is centered around the murders of the Clutter family, who lived on a large farm in Holcomb, Kansas. Capote goes into great detail in describing the Clutter home and the tree-lined lane leading to the house where the murders took place. My mother was determined to see that house for herself. And we found the Clutter farmhouse exactly as Capote described.

But my mother was not yet satisfied. Which should not come as a surprise to anyone who knew her. She wanted to find the cemetery where the Clutter family was buried, but we had no idea where it might be. She badgered my father to stop, against his will, at a local gas station and ask for directions. We found the cemetery and the Clutter family graves.

Strangely enough, I undertook a similar journey of my own to Savannah years later after reading *Midnight in the Garden of Good and Evil*.

Chapter 8

2014

Jan 2 - My Surgeon: "All things considered, you're in remarkably good shape for your age." Me: "Are you sure you're in the right room?"

Feb 25 - This debate in Arizona and other states about allowing businesses to refuse service to people because their lifestyle might in some way go against your personal religious beliefs, reminds me of that very famous quote by the Rev. Martin Niemoller who was trying to explain how Hitler and the Nazis were able to come to power and take control in Germany. Rev. Niemoller said the following:

"First, they came for the Socialists and I did not speak out, because I was not a Socialist.

"Then they came for the Trade Unionists and I did not speak out, because I was not a Trade Unionist.

"Then they came for the Jews and I did not speak out, because I was not a Jew.

"Then they came for me and there was no one left to speak out."

Rev. Niemoller was a prominent Protestant minister and outspoken foe of Hitler. Niemoller spent the last 7 years of Nazi rule in concentration camps.

Today the target for 'legal discrimination' may be gays and lesbians, but if this effort is successful, who will become the target next month or next year??

March 15 - Since, especially at my age, there is not a great deal I can do about the quantity of life I may have remaining, I have decided that I should focus more on quality. That will mean some changes and, hopefully, more fun, sun and laughter.

March 18 - My closest and dearest friend is leaving Louisville for good tomorrow. He has been there for me through everything, good and bad. After my heart attack and all the terrible complications that followed, he was always there for me. My recovery would have never happened if he had not helped and pushed me when I needed it. I owe him everything and there are no words that can adequately express my appreciation.

April 1 - 40 years ago, I spent the better part of 1974 as a VISTA volunteer in the small Appalachian coal town of Wheelwright Kentucky. Vista or Volunteers in Service to America was essentially the American branch of the Peace Corps.

Wheelwright was a small 'coal camp town' built in 1916 by the Elkhorn Coal Company. At one time, Wheelwright was considered a 'model town' and included its own high school, hospital, swimming pool, tennis courts, 9-hole golf course and company owned stores. Every single structure in the town was owned by the coal company. In the prosperous times of the 1930s and 1940s the town boasted a population of a little over 2,000. All the miners rented their homes from the company and bought their goods in the company store.

Wheelwright was also widely known as one of the regional headquarters of the 'pack horse' library, which was a WPA program that operated from 1935 to 1943. Librarians, largely women, delivered books to remote areas of Appalachia on horseback. When the coal reserves began to dwindle the town was eventually sold to the Island Creek Coal Company which had virtually no interest in maintaining it. Wheelwright began to fall into disrepair and when the mine was closed in 1972; the population plummeted as people abandoned the town to seek work elsewhere.

In the mid-70s the University of Kentucky in conjunction with VISTA sent a team of volunteer students to assist in organizing the local residents and officials to fight back and persuade the absentee owners to either move to restore the town or, at least, sell the homes to those residents who wished to purchase the houses they'd been renting. The residents were, for the most part, warm and welcoming. I was one of a handful of students chosen for this project and I spent nearly a year working with town officials and a local attorney to enact a series or new ordinances and a housing code in an effort to convince the absentee owner to take a greater interest in repairing and maintaining the town and its homes. Eventually the entire town was sold to the Kentucky Housing Authority which did undertake to rehabilitate the homes and offer them for sale to local residents. As of the 2010 Census, Wheelwright had a population of 780.

Today the history, even the very existence of these early 'coal camps' has been largely forgotten. But I remember the town and its warm and determined people.

April 9 - A very emotional day something I have been wanting to do for a long time, I stopped by the Nashville hospital where I very nearly died to see and thank the folks there who cared for me and literally saved my life. They were surprised and happy to see me. The doctor who heads up the ICU recognized me right away. He was smiling from ear to ear and gave me a big hug. They were happy to see me doing so well and I was glad to finally say thank you in person.

April 28 - Today I walked in the footsteps of giants and experienced history up close and personal. I visited the Gold Coast Railroad Museum in Miami, just across the way from the Miami Zoo. History was heavy in the air.

The museum is now home to the historic 'Ferdinand Magellan' rail car. It is Pullman rail car first constructed in 1929. But in 1943 it underwent a major refurbishment and upgrade to serve as the official Presidential Rail Car for Franklin Roosevelt. President Roosevelt used it until his death in 1945. It is also the site of one of the most famous photographs of 20th century American history. It is where, in 1948, President Harry Truman held up a copy of the Chicago Daily Tribune newspaper with the bold headline proclaiming "Dewey Defeats Truman".

Today visitors can tour the car and view the room used for presidential meetings, Roosevelt's bedroom and the kitchen area. Of particular interest were the very thick, bulletproof glass windows.

The Ferdinand Magellan remained in Presidential service until 1958. In 1985 it was designated a National Historic Landmark.

June 14 - While. taking a short break from packing, I suddenly realized that one week from tomorrow I will turn 60, and 2 weeks from tomorrow I will leave behind Louisville, my home town for the past 60 years in order to head to warm and sunny south Florida. Those are some pretty big changes all at once, but, I also realized that I am a fighter, I am a survivor and I will 'endeavor to persevere'.

July 1 - The Alaska cruise, 5 years ago this month and my first-ever cruise, was ostensibly to celebrate my retirement from state government, even though I was only 54 years old. But my true motive was hidden and not what you might expect.

I had been a huge fan of the TV series Northern Exposure since it first aired in 1990. It ran for 5 years and a total of 110 episodes. It won 27 awards including the Emmy for Best Prime Time Drama. It was essentially a 'fish out of water' type story with a quirky cast of unusually odd characters. One of the characters was the town itself. The fictional setting for the show was Cicely, Alaska but it was actually filmed largely in the town of Roslyn, Washington, which is only about an hour and a half drive from Seattle where my cruise originated. And I made sure our scheduling allowed time after the cruise for a visit to Roslyn (Cicely). It was a spectacular visit and the town appeared exactly as it did on TV. We visited The Brick a real operating local restaurant/bar that featured prominently in the series. We were also able to stop by the doctor's office and KBHR, the town's fictional radio station. But perhaps the most meaningful and most moving of all was visiting Ruth Ann's small general store where so much happened in the series. An actual store and gift shop was operating in the store front space that had been used for the TV series. Upon walking through the door into 'Ruth Ann's store' I was overcome with emotion and began to cry. I loved the show and the quirky characters and was truly overjoyed to be able to visit their town and walk in their shoes. It still moves me to day when I recall it. The cruise was nice too.

Aug 10 - Today it was 94 degrees here in south Florida and I went to the beach on Key Biscayne. Weekends are not a great time to visit the beach here, very crowded and noisy. I only stayed an hour or so, but I will go back soon. Being on Key Biscayne brought back memories of Richard Nixon: I remember him clearly and know exactly where I was when he resigned, 40 years ago. Like many politicians, at his core, I think he was a terribly insecure person. That was all so long ago, it feels now like something I saw in a movie. It's hard to believe that I actually lived through those very troubled times.

Oct 4 - Sometimes it's difficult to know whether you are chasing something or running from something. But whatever the case may be, just remember, don't look back.

Oct 19 - Just a few seconds of insane courage can change your life forever. We all, I believe, have that courage somewhere within us, we just have to find it and believe in ourselves even if no one else does, no matter our destination, it is the journey that shapes us and how we make it will define who we are.

Nov 9 - Sometimes certain aspects of life, even life itself, can be hard, but I am always reminded of that great Tom Hanks line from "A League of Their Own": "It's supposed to be hard, if it wasn't hard every one would do it, the 'hard' is what makes it great." It may sound corny, but that line has helped me get through some tough times, and then I think of that other great line that always brings a smile to my face.

Nov 11 - Thinking about my father today on Veterans Day, he passed away several years ago. He fought in Korea, was part of a tank crew, was wounded in battle and awarded the Purple Heart. He did not talk about his war experiences much, but what I remember most is his recounting how incredibly cold it was there and how hard it was to operate in below zero weather. I wish he had lived long enough to see little ol' Terry from Shively training grizzly bears and tigers. He would have loved that.

Nov 24 - Watching news reports about several recent high-profile trials dredged up a deeply buried memory from decades ago.

In the 80s I was summoned for jury duty and ended up on a jury considering a murder case. The prosecutor was Ernie Jasmine, who some Louisville folks may remember. The trial lasted about a day and a half and I was chosen as jury foreman since I made the mistake of speaking first once we got into the jury room. All I said was that maybe we should take a vote before we began because it might be that we all agreed on a verdict without much discussion. Everyone thought that sounded like a good idea, but of course we did not agree. I think 10 voted guilty and 1 not guilty and 1 undecided. To me it was pretty clear cut. A guy got into an argument with his lady friend in a car and shot her 4 or 5 times. His defense attorney argued that the gun went off as they struggled for it. But 4 or 5 times?? And witnesses also reported that he chased her down the sidewalk as she fled from the car.

After about 2 hours of discussion, we all agreed on a guilty verdict, which I as foreman had to present to the judge. It all went fine; everyone was calm and cool. All the formalities were completed, the judged thanked us for our service and ordered the bailiffs to keep everyone confined to the courtroom until all the jurors had safely left the building ... not a memory I like to replay very often.

Dec 18 - I say the words, "I don't know" more often than almost anyone I know and the older I get, the more often I say it. I'm not sure if that means I'm dumber or just more honest ...I just don't know…

Chapter 9

2013

April 1 - My first real job, just out of college, was in downtown Louisville in the late 70s. I clearly remember that most of the men wore suits and ties and a good many of the men still wore hats with their suits. That's one fashion trend I'm glad to see fade away.

May 1 - While working at the Zoo there was one thing in particular, I could never quite get straight in my mind. The Zoo had a very dedicated and passionate head veterinarian. And very often if a medical problem arose, he didn't walk or even use a golf cart to get to the scene. He ran, often sprinting to the site where his assistance was needed.

Now it can be somewhat disconcerting to be working away at a zoo and look up only to see the head veterinarian sprinting full out across the zoo grounds. You never quite know for sure if you should follow after him to provide any needed assistance or run for your life in the opposite direction.

May 4 - It has been 40 years since the greatest race horse of all time, Secretariat, set a Derby record that still stands today and went on to win the Triple Crown. One of the most memorable birthday presents I've ever received was from a friend who surprised me with a tour of the horse farm in Lexington where Secretariat spent his retirement years. We got to see 'Big Red' up close. That's something you never forget.

May 10 - Lennie McLaughlin ... recognize the name? Probably not but probably should. Miss Lennie, as she was known, was an influential Democratic political "boss" right here in Louisville, Kentucky during the 40s, 50s and 60s. She was one of only a handful of women "political bosses" in the entire country and she reigned right here in Louisville. Just one of the many who have gone before us who we should not forget. I may share a few more between now and election day - Gerta Bendl, Mae Street Kidd, Georgia Powers and Thelma Stovall.

May 15 - The historic Watergate hearings into President Richard Nixon's 1972 reelection campaign against Senator George McGovern took place this month, 40 years ago. The Congressional hearings, broadcast live on national television focused on the burglary of the Democratic National Committee offices in the Watergate building in downtown Washington, D.C. and the involvement of Richard Nixon.

I had a close-up view of the hearings as it was the summer I was serving as an intern in the Washington office of Kentucky Senator Marlow Cook. In fact, my brush with history began on my first day, even before I made my way to Senator Cook's office. I found myself on the sidewalk outside the Old Senate Office Building, where the hearings were being held and where Senator Cook's office was located. As I was waiting to cross the street, I stood next to a short man with a bow tie, later when I saw his photo on the front page of the Washington Post I realized I had been standing next to prosecutor Archibald Cox.

The hearings were conducted in the Old Senate Office Building where Senator Cook's office was located, just down the hall from Senator Sam Irvin who served as chairman of the Watergate investigation committee. As a Senate intern I was able to go in and out of the hearing room to watch the hearings from a special section roped off for Congressional staff in the back of the room.

Even though there was an air of high drama and history, no one could foresee that the hearings and the revelations they produced would lead to President Richard Nixon resigning from office in August of 1974. The first and only American President to ever resign from office.

June 12 - Ok, frequently I hear people say, 'I'm not interested in history' or 'I never liked history in school' and always I think to myself, 'you are an idiot'. I try hard not to say this out loud. You don't have to be a genius to figure out that if you don't know anything about the past which has brought us to where we are now, then you have no intelligent idea on how to make a better future for YOURSELF, your family or your country.

June 13 - I don't know whatever happened to the people who tainted the Tylenol bottles back in the early 80s. I don't think they were ever caught. But I hope they have had miserable, unhappy lives because they are responsible for the fiasco we now call 'tamper free' or 'childproof' packaging. Oh, you can say it's because I am getting old that I now require a box cutter of some sort just to open that package of pretzels I bought. But I know things were not this difficult to open back when I was a kid. It's not just medicine bottles you have to squeeze or align, but those 'press here to open' boxes that you simply crush when you 'press here'. If we can send men to the moon, surely, it can't be that difficult to devise packaging that doesn't' require a lethally sharp instrument of death to open. Today's rant was brought to you by Velveeta Shells and Cheese.

June 14 – I have been using a new rehabilitation technique and it seems to be doing wonders for me. It is very much like shopping. In fact, it is shopping. It is a good physical and mental workout the comparison shopping, the planning ahead for fall and winter, so much to consider, so many comparisons to be thought through. Most of my purchases are not that significant, just a couple of things here and there, mostly Target. Interestingly, most of my 'significant' purchases were not planned, just happened upon a really good deal while working on my 'rehab', like that Michael Koors cashmere overcoat. I don't have a lot of designer clothes, but I have a few more now and, of course, I HAD to get that remote control toy helicopter - after all, my birthday is almost here and the dog ate my other one (seriously, ask Eric). This rehab business is serious and tough, but I have nicer clothes and more fun toys.

June 20 - Recently I bought a new fancy, Lawn Boy, self-propelled lawnmower and a few weeks later, I bought a new GPS on sale at Target. So, (you do see where this is going, right?) I have been wondering if there is some way to hook up my GPS to my self-propelled lawnmower. It could be kinda like one of those Roomba vacuums.

July 27 - It's been 25 years since I was a delegate to the Democratic National Convention in Atlanta in 1988. People ask me what I remember most about that convention and that's an easy one. At the time it was exciting, but later it would become one of the most poignant and moving episodes of my life. One evening, as speakers droned on and on, I looked around the upper sections of seats behind where the Kentucky delegation was seated and I spotted a well-dressed, handsome young guy sitting by himself in a dimly lit row of seats. As my eyes adjusted and the figure came into focus, I realized I was looking at John Kennedy, Jr. He had apparently sought out a quiet, out of the way spot for a respite from reporters and autograph seekers

Later, as I was returning to my seat from a trip to the concession stand, I ran into him in the tunnel leading to the convention floor. I said hello and remarked that it was a pleasure to meet him, he thanked me and stopped to ask where I was from and my name. He was very gracious and kind.

I saw him several times that week and was always impressed by how kind and patient he was with all the people who wanted to shake his hand, get his autograph, or have a picture taken with him. He was always obliging but I will always remember him sitting alone in the dimly-lit, upper rows of the arena looking for a little reprieve from the spotlight.

Dec 15 - Christmas has long been my favorite time of year. In fact, friends know that I leave a small pencil-type Christmas tree up year-round. I just enjoy looking at all the pretty colored lights especially during the dark days of winter. But one of my most enduring Christmas memories has nothing to do with the spirit of the season.

One dreary December day while working in Frankfort, my coworker and friend Leslie Brown and I decided to do a little last minute Christmas shopping during our lunch hour. We headed out to the local Elder Beerman store not far from our office.

Leslie was actually shopping while I was mostly just killing time. But I did spot one item which piqued my interest. It was a chair equipped with heat and massage and a large sign reading 'Give Me a Try'. It sounded like a good idea to me. So, I sat in the chair to 'Gve it a Try' as the sign instructed.

Almost immediately a store clerk approached me saying, "Get up." I looked at him in disbelief and again he said, more adamantly this time, "Get up."

Thinking that he was unaware that I was simply following directions or that perhaps he was just being rude, I replied, somewhat stridently, "Excuse me." And again, he barked at me, "Get up." About this time, I spotted my friend Leslie walking toward me laughing so hard she was unable to speak. So, I got up and walked over to her and asked, "What's going on?"

"He was telling you to get up because fire was shooting out your butt." She managed to mutter through her laughter.

Apparently, a leg of the chair was sitting on the electrical cord powering the massage and heat features and when I sat down sparks and flames came shooting out from underneath the chair in all directions. Of course, I was totally oblivious. I could not see any of this as it was happening.

Only Leslie and the store clerk saw the sparks and flames 'shooting out' from my backside. But I did see the scorch marks on the floor after Leslie and I finally got our laughter under control. Such wonderful Christmas memories.

Chapter 10

2012

Jan 3 - How can all these 'leading economists' keep saying we have a 'service economy' when we have to pump our own gas and ring up our own groceries?

Jan 26 - Every day we come to a fork in the road. If we take the high road, we not only meet like-minded friends, we meet good people who look and think and believe differently. We can learn from them, and them from us. But if we take the low road, all we encounter is hatred, ignorance, fear, prejudice and anger. Every time I find myself on the low road, I try to reset my GPS device and get back to where I need to be.

Feb 15 - Back in 1987 I went to visit a friend from Louisville who had relocated to Las Vegas. We had a great time hitting the casinos and quite a few of the slot machines. But the most amazing thing happened entirely by accident.

We wanted to see Caesar's Palace and when we walked into the main casino, we were flabbergasted to find a movie film crew hard at work. We had arrived just in time to witness the iconic scene where Tom Cruise and Dustin Hoffman come down the escalator to the main floor of the casino. Of course, the movie was Rain Man which went on to win 4 Academy Awards, including Best Picture and Best Actor (Dustin Hoffman).

April 25 - Okay, so I decided it was a nice afternoon for a bike ride. My bike had been in the back of the garage all winter and, of course, the tires were flat. I had to use a hand pump to inflate the tires. You see where this is going, right?? By the time I had pumped the tires full of air, I was too tired to go riding. Good intentions and all that.

April 26 - I have to say that I really don't like all the talk about a "bucket list". The whole focus is all wrong. I have a list, have had one since high school, but it is a "life list", because it's all about how you want to live your life to the fullest, not about getting things done before you die. I've been very fortunate to do a lot of things on my "life list" but there are still many waiting and I'm still working on them every day.

June 20 - When we are young, we cannot yet imagine the joys or the tragedies that life has in store for us. When we are older, if we are lucky, we learn to appreciate and accept both with grace. Thank you to all my friends who watch out for me every day. I see you doing it and I am grateful.

June 24 - It's hard to believe it was 50 years ago today, but as far back as I can remember, I have loved baseball, playing it, watching it in person, especially watching it in old stadiums, like the one in Evansville or Fenway Park, even the old Yankee Stadium. I think it probably has a lot to do with my Dad, who was also my Little League coach back when I played baseball, I think he must have loved it too. After all, I remember him taking us to a Yankees/ Detroit game when we went to New York on vacation, in 1962. And I got to see Mickey Mantle, Roger Maris and Yogi Berra. The game lasted for 22 innings, 7 hours, and was the longest major league game ever played at that time. The Yankees ended up winning 9-7 and Marris scored 2 runs while Mantle scored 1 that day. Thanks Dad, I have never forgotten that. All those memories came flooding over me today when I saw that Don Zimmer had passed away. If you know baseball, then you know Don Zimmer, if not, there is no way I would know how to explain it all but thanks Don and thanks Dad. I will miss you both.

July 4 - What a fortunate person I am. I spent one Fourth of July on the Mall in Washington D.C. along with a million others watching the Beach Boys; I spent another Fourth in Boston on the banks of the Charles River listening to the Boston Pops; and in 1986 I spent the Fourth in New York watching the tall ships from around the world celebrating the rededication of the Statue of liberty.

July 5 - I try to do the right thing, I try to do it the right way and I try to speak ill of no one (usually). If others choose to find fault, be negative and criticize, then so be it, that is their shortcoming not mine.

July 8 - Sometimes I feel like I'm just impersonating myself.

Aug 4 - Life is not measured by the number of breaths we take but by the moments that take our breath away.

Aug 30 - Churchill Downs is one of the most historic race tracks in America, perhaps the world. But my favorite spot is a place the general public rarely sees. It is a small restaurant on the backside of the track, near the horse barns. It is the place many of the exercise riders and jockeys go to eat after their morning workouts. The food is good and relatively cheap. But that is not why I like it so much. With so many jockeys and exercise riders all around it is the only time I ever get to be the tallest guy in the room.

Sept 5 - I keep seeing people who say they want to "take America back" and I keep wondering, back to what? As for myself, I'm much more interested in moving my country forward as an innovative, inspiring world leader.

Sept 6 - And while I'm at it, I am sick and tired of hearing people trash the 'intellectual elite'. I'm no intellectual, but when did being smart or having a good education become something to be ridiculed? I'm pretty sure that Jefferson, Madison, Franklin, Adams and the others were the "intellectual elite' of their time. I don't know whether they were liberal or conservative, but one thing is undeniable, they were all revolutionaries. We should all be thankful they were.

Nov 26 - A personal suggestion - should you find yourself feeling that life seems to be beating you down and that daily struggles are becoming too much for you to handle, set aside some time to watch the movie, The King's Speech. This inspiring, true story demonstrates that no matter our status or station in life, we all face difficulties and challenges, but if we can summon the strength and courage to persevere and meet the challenges head on, we can survive and even triumph. Believe me, I know.

Dec 5 - There's no limit to what you can accomplish in life, if you don't care who gets the credit.

Dec 27 – "Success is not final; failure is not fatal; it is the courage to continue that counts." Winston Churchill

Dec 28 – The important thing in life is not how many times you may be knocked down. The important thing is how many times you get up, dust yourself off and move forward.

About the Author

Terry Feathers is lifelong political activist who, for over 5 decades worked as a campaign adviser, manager, speechwriter and consultant for over 50 campaigns. He worked in Louisville City Hall, the Kentucky General Assembly and the Kentucky Court of Justice and in Washington, D.C. He served as the Government Affairs Manager for the Louisville Chamber of Commerce where he directed a successful statewide campaign to amend the Kentucky Constitution. He was an elected delegate to the 1988 Democratic National Convention in Atlanta.

He is a graduate of the University of Kentucky and studied government and American political history at Harvard University. While at the University of Kentucky he served as an intern in the U. S. Senate in Washing, D, C. Additionally, he has studied at various times at the University of Louisville and Bellarmine University.

From 2006-2012 he worked and volunteered at the Louisville Zoo helping care for and train a wide variety of exotic animals including lions, tigers and bears.

He is a co-author and editor of A Decade of Progress for Kentucky Courts (1993).

Made in the USA
Monee, IL
23 November 2022

18402765R00080